THE GREEK ISLANDS

Fisherfolk of Spetsai; fishing is the way of life of most of the Greek islanders.

THIS BEAUTIFUL WORLD   VOL. 27

THE GREEK ISLANDS

by DEREK A. C. DAVIES

 KODANSHA INTERNATIONAL LTD.
TOKYO, NEW YORK & SAN FRANCISCO

Distributed in the United States by Kodansha International/USA Ltd. through Harper & Row, Publishers, Inc., 10 East 53rd Street, New York, New York 10022.

Published by Kodansha International Ltd., 12-21, Otowa 2-chome, Bunkyo-ku, Tokyo 112 and Kodansha International/ USA Ltd., 10 East 53rd Street, New York, New York 10022 and 44 Montgomery Street, San Francisco, California 94104. Copyright © 1971 by Kodansha International Ltd. All rights reserved. Printed in Japan.

LCC 73–158639
ISBN 0–87011–154–x
JBC 0326–783038–2361

First edition, 1971
Fifth printing, 1981

Contents

Island of the Saint 7
Devil's Island 17
Island of the Knights 25
The Great Island 30
The Circle of Islands 75
The Far Island 100
Map 102

For Sumiko

Happy is the man who, before dying, has the good fortune to sail the Aegean Sea. Nowhere else can one pass so easily and serenely from reality to dream.

Nikos Kazantzakis
Zorba the Greek

Island of the Saint

I had always pictured Corfu as an island basking in bright sunlight, its rugged cliffs plunging into a peacock blue sea and the fragrance of lemons, pine, and herbs trailing in the air. As it turned out, a thin rain was falling as we approached, and the island was a gray silhouette against a pale sky. Little was visible except the somber façade of tall houses on the waterfront and two grim forts. The Venus of the Isles, it depressed me to see, was not at her best in early April.

On the quay to meet the boat were a number of taxis, horse-drawn victoria cabs and porters with large wooden handcarts, one of whom guided my heavy suitcase along the waterfront towards the Hotel Cyprus in the old quarter of the town. It was a typical Mediterranean scene, with small boats being loaded and unloaded and fishermen mending their nets on the wharf. The old porter was friendly and inquisitive: where did I come from? Where was I going? How did I like Greece? Although our conversation was limited by his sparse knowledge of English and mine of Greek, I felt an inexplicable sense of freedom and ease. I was going to enjoy Greece in spite of the weather.

We made our way up into the old quarter. Tall houses, their

THE GREEK ISLANDS 🌀🌀

plaster walls crumbling and shutters battered, lean at odd angles as if nodding to each other across the narrow, cobbled streets. Small shops and open-air stalls spill over with fish and fruit, meat and vegetables. Donkeys plod about laden with heavy, wooden baskets; bearded priests in black hats and robes stalk by. Crones wearing black head scarfs amble along, crumpled over their wooden sticks. The number of cats scavenging or scuttling down alleyways like the rats of Hamlin seemed extraordinary.

It is said that if you shout the name "Spiros" in the streets of Corfu at least twenty men will come running; the reason is that nearly half the male population of the island is named after Saint Spyridon, the patron saint. The Corfiots have a great respect for their saint, whose mummified body lies in a beautiful glass-topped silver casket in the Church of Saint Spyridon, and four times a year he is carried in splendid procession round the town. Each day a stream of people files past the casket like Moscovites paying their respects at the tomb of Lenin. They kiss the saint's feet, which protrude from one end of the casket, and they kiss all the sacred icons on the walls—indeed so profuse are they with their kisses that it is said that if there were a disease on the island, within a few days everyone would be infected.

At the church door one can buy a list of Saint Spyridon's miracles, which shows that, since he came to Corfu from Cyprus in 1460, he has worked hard for his adopted island. Curing common colds and epilepsy, helping fishing boats through bad storms—they are all in a day's work for the saint. Perhaps his greatest miracle was his changing himself into a squall and driving away a fleet of invading Turks.

Thus Corfu never came under the domination of Turkey, as

ISLAND OF THE SAINT

did the rest of Greece, most of which was part of the Ottoman Empire for nearly three centuries. But the saint did not drive away the Venetians; indeed, they had been welcomed as a protecting power against pirates, and they gave the island its name. The Venetians stayed for four centuries (1386-1797) and left behind many fine buildings, two strong forts—which today dominate the east and west points of the town—and stamped an unmistakable Italian character on the island and its people.

After the saint, a second important Corfu institution is cricket. The game is played in the large main square and in the back streets as it is played anywhere in England, with the exception of some small variations in rules and style. *Oudatt*, for instance, in Corfu cricket means "out" (in England the expression might be heard as a dialect variation of "How's that?"). And whereas the English batsman tries to play the game with the bat held vertically, the Corfiot tends to swing horizontally, enthusiastically and not always accurately. This is a hangover, so it is said, from the days when cricket bats were curved.

Cricket in Corfu? For a short period the Ionian Islands, of which Corfu is the best known and the most densely populated, were a British protectorate. Traces of the British stay, which lasted from 1814 to 1864, are evident in a few fine buildings—including the house in which the present Duke of Edinburgh was born—and the Corfiot taste for ginger beer.

Britain was not the only country to take a fancy to Corfu; indeed, the island was a pawn in the European power game for centuries. Originally said to be an island of the Phoenicians, it was colonized by the Corinthians in 734 B.C. and successively conquered or sacked by the Spartans, Pharians, Romans (229 B.C.), Vandals, Goths,

THE GREEK ISLANDS 🌀🌀

Sicilians, Venetians, French, Russians, British, Italians (1923, 1940–43), and Germans (1943–45). Considering this history of oppression, it is surprising that the island has remained Greek at all, and that the people are so easygoing, friendly and pleasure loving.

During my stay on the island, I frequented a small *taverna* hidden in the maze of back alleys. The dim, rather dirty room was illuminated by a naked electric light bulb, and about a dozen bare-topped tables and barrels of wine lined the walls. In one corner was a large, primitive oven, on top of which were large copper cauldrons of food: *mousaka*, haricot beans, large stuffed tomatoes, stuffed vine leaves, and various other Greek foods. In Greece, the easiest way to order at a restaurant if you do not know the names of the dishes is to go into the kitchen and look into the pots.

Here I had my first taste of *ouzo*, the Greek aniseed spirit (similar in flavor to the French pernod), and *retsina*. Most Greek wines taste of the resin used to caulk the barrels, and the Greeks believe that it is good for the digestion as well as the palate. Foreigners tend to disagree, though I soon aquired a taste for it and found *retsina* particularly thirst quenching on hot days. Drinks are always served with *mezethes*, savory snacks consisting of a choice of cheese, olives, slices of tomatoes, squid, artichoke, or whatever else is available. In the country, where vegetables are plentiful, *mezethes* can be almost a meal in themselves. There are many fine potables, and they are popular, but it is rare to see a Greek very drunk. One suspects that even today the ancient axiom of Greek philosophy "everything in moderation" is still the guiding maxim.

The proprietor of the *taverna* was a fat, cheery man known as Onassis, who had a friendly word for everyone. He enjoyed teaching me the various toasts, his favorite being *aspro parto* ("white

ISLAND OF THE SAINT

bottoms") which is, obviously, the equivalent of "bottoms up." He also explained that his countrymen always clink glasses when they drink so that all the senses—taste, sight, smell, touch, and finally sound—are employed while drinking.

Onassis seemed to regard his *taverna* more as an evening gathering of his friends than as a business, and frequently he would forget that there were other customers that might want to be served. I learned that in Greece you are not expected to sit shyly at a table waiting to be asked what you want; you shout or bang a fork on the table to get service.

If a stranger enters a pub in England he is almost always met with indifference. Not so in Greece; at Onassis's *taverna* people, mostly sailors and fishermen, were friendly, curious and often so generous that it became impossible to pay for drinks. I also met a plumber there who was anxious to learn English; I taught him for a time, and in return he taught me Greek. His name, by the way, was Sophocles.

The *taverna*, like most Greek institutions, is ancient, and there are many different types, from those with chic decor, expensive food, and a dance band to bare rooms with sawdust on the floor. But wherever it is, when a man or a group gets up to dance it can be a memorable sight. If the dance is good, the audience responds with plates and glasses—thrown crashing at the feet of the dancers. This practice is against the law now, but it still continues.

> *Be not afeard: the isle is full of noises,*
> *Sounds and sweet airs that give delight and hurt not.*

With these words Shakespeare described Prospero's island in *The Tempest*, and it has been suggested that it was Corfu that he had in mind. Certainly his poetry fits the gentle, haunting mood of the

11

THE GREEK ISLANDS

island, as I found out when I set out to explore the countryside, heading for the village of Sinardes, on a rented motorbike.

By April the rains of winter have saturated the island and the spring flowers and purple Judas trees are bright explosions of color amidst the lush green. Silver-green olive leaves flicker in the wind, while stately cypresses gaze aristocratically over the orchards. Swallows en route to northern Europe wheel and spin in the air, which is heavy with the scent of fruit and flowers.

Near Sinardes, the road becomes rough and steep and passes through a forest of tall olive trees, their tortured trunks and branches testifying to their age, some perhaps three or four hundred years old. Olive trees are of great value in Greece and are a measure of both a man's wealth and the size of a bride's dowry. On Corfu alone there are about three and one-half million trees.

When I got to the village, I was reminded of a Corfiot proverb: "Women should be beaten like an olive tree, but in Corfu neither the women nor the olive trees are beaten—because of the terrible laziness of everyone." A number of men, most of them old and some of them wearing the traditional costume of a black head scarf and baggy pants, were sitting at the tables outside the old café. They clicked their inevitable worry-beads and nursed thimble-sized cups of heavily sedimented Turkish coffee. They studied me with interest as I propped the motorbike up against a wall and sat down at a table. With the usual Greek generosity somebody bought me a coffee. There were the usual friendly questions.

One old man offered to show me the village. We walked down the main street where the houses are painted yellow ochre and the door frames white, and where woven rugs were hanging out of the windows to air. Women seemed to be doing all the work; on their

ISLAND OF THE SAINT

heads they carried wicker baskets of olives to the oil magazine, where the last of the crop was being crushed into olive oil. It was a dimly lit building with a stamped earth floor, full of modern electrical presses and grinders; until recently, ponies were used for power. The olives are given a preliminary mashing in a large metal bin, and then the pulp is transferred to a second press where it is crushed between layers of what looked like burlap. Hot water filters through this second press to speed the flow of the oil, which is then collected in large vats and left to settle. Olive oil accounts for over half the gross product of Corfu.

In Sinardes many people wanted to have their photograph taken. As soon as I raised my camera, a group would pose before it, smiling expectantly; these do not always make the best photographs. One man insisted that I photograph him holding a picture of his dead son. I have no idea why. Another wanted me to take him reading a newspaper, an uncommon ability in a remote area of a country where the literacy rate is low. By the time I left the village my notebook was filled with the names of people to whom I had promised to send pictures.

It was beginning to rain when I reached the Achilleion Palace on the other side of the island—appropriate conditions, perhaps, for the Achilleion story. It was commissioned in the late nineteenth century by the empress Elizabeth of Austria, who wanted a palace "with pillared colonnades and hanging gardens, protected from prying glances—a palace worthy of Achilles." The result was a pretentious building in neoclassical style, with couches covered with leopard skins, marble baths filled with warm sea water, and terraced gardens crowded with imitations of classical sculpture. Elizabeth, estranged from her husband, came to Corfu hoping to find some

THE GREEK ISLANDS

comfort on the island that she considered "the most beautiful place in the world." But she was never happy. Her only son committed suicide shortly before the palace was completed, and Elizabeth herself died at the hands of an assassin in 1898. Her statue stands in the woods below the palace, looking out over the hills of Albania. She seems sad, frustrated, and lonely; I am sure she would not be any happier to know that today her palace is used as a casino.

Like most of the Greek islands, Corfu's early history is shrouded in myth. By tradition it is the home of the Phaeacians where Odysseus was shipwrecked and where he surprised the Princess Nausicaa and her maids by appearing in front of them naked and unkempt, "his skin bleached and worn like an old sea shell." The girls fled in terror from this startling sight—all except the beautiful princess who stayed to talk to this man whom she described "like the gods who live in the heaven ... the kind of man I would fancy for a husband." But the lovely Nausicaa was unlucky. Odysseus was married already, and after staying the night at the palace of King Alcinous, Nausicaa's father, the king's men escorted him home to the island of Ithaca, which is about seventy miles south of Corfu, and thus he ended his ten years of wandering.

Notwithstanding the efforts of archeologists, the site of Alcinous's palace has not been found, but it is thought that Odysseus landed near the cliffs of Palaiokastritsa. It is surprising that Homer makes no mention of the beauty of this place, which can best be seen from the hills or from the courtyard of the monastery just above Palaiokastritsa ("Old Castle"). The muffled roar of the waves echoes up from the foot of the cliffs, and promontories of the northwest coast of the island stretch out into the haze like jagged red teeth set into a sea of solid blue marble. It is probably the most beautiful spot

ISLAND OF THE SAINT

in Corfu, and the monks could scarcely have chosen a better place to contem plate the absolute.

A flat tire brought my tour of the island to a premature end on a lonely stretch of impossibly bad road somewhere between Palaiokastritsa and Pelekas. There was no garage within ten miles, and I resigned myself to a long walk back to Corfu wheeling the motorbike. Fortunately a truck laden with hay came along and stopped beside me. Without waiting for any explanation, the driver jumped down and started to haul the motorbike on top of the hay. Thus I arrived back in Corfu (the Greeks call the island Kerkira); the name applies both to the island and the town, as is so often the case in Greek.

I had one more ride on a motorbike before I left the island. It was late evening in Onassis' *taverna* and I was talking to Spiros, a young student who was about to begin his studies at an Italian university. Early the next morning I was to take the ferry to Igoumenitsa on the mainland and thence go by bus to Athens.

"If you want to come back one day to Corfu," said Spiros, "you must drink from the fountain at Kakardi. We have a belief that anyone who drinks this water will return one day."

Of course I wanted to come back: there was so much more I wanted to see, so much more time I would have to spend inland. But it was late, and I had to get up early the next morning.

The decision was made for me. Spiros jumped up. "Come on," he said, "we'll go now, by motorbike."

I recognized the road to Kanoni as we sped out of Corfu in the dark. As we took a corner much to fast for my liking, Spiros shouted blithely over his shoulder, "Two months ago my friend crashed here on his motorbike. He was killed." I feared we might share that fate.

THE GREEK ISLANDS 🌀🌀

In a quarter of an hour we were on a hill overlooking the black night sea. "This is where I bring my girl friends during the summer," Spiros remarked, as we climbed down a steep path to the beach. The water flowed from a fountain onto the rocks. I drank it thirstily and splashed it on my face.

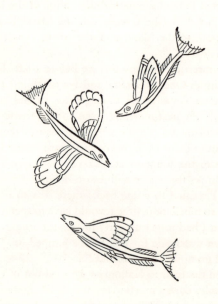

Devil's Island

The Aegean islands are linked to Piraeus, the port city of Athens, by fleets of ferry boats of assorted ages, shapes, sizes, reliability, comfort, prices and speeds. Schedules are extraordinarily complicated and frequently unreliable, and one's first impression is that destinations and departure times are decided a few hours before a boat leaves, entirely at the whim of the captain. Before setting out for Santorin ("Devil's Island") I asked four different shipping agents in Athens for the day and time of departure and was given four different answers. Eventually a Greek friend referred to a daily newspaper where the shipping schedule—rather to my surprise—proved accurate.

The port of Piraeus is large and busy, and there is an air of excitement and expectation in the crowds that cluster like flies alongside the steamers. Up the narrow gangplanks come peasant women in black shawls carrying battered suitcases, baskets of poultry, brown paper parcels, babies, bunches of vine leaves, and a hundred other assorted bundles. Bearded hitchhikers struggle with heavy rucksacks, tourists flash expensive cameras, and soldiers wave good-bye to their girl friends. On the quay photographers with old-fashioned box cameras and black cloths take souvenir snaps, while on board

THE GREEK ISLANDS

white-coated peddlers sell various things for the voyage: bread, drinks, sunglasses, plastic toys, suntan oil, polythene bags, and lemons to be sucked in case of seasickness. None of the islands is more than twenty-four hours away from Piraeus, but it seemed to me that the islanders treat the voyage as if it were a major expedition —and indeed, for some the trip to and from Athens might be a once-in-a-lifetime event.

On most ferries there are four classes, from first, where one has almost complete privacy, to deck, which can be as crowded as a popular *taverna* on a Sunday night and where the best place to sleep is curled up in a sleeping bag underneath the lifeboats. That is how I traveled to Santorin on board the M.S. *Mioulis*, a fifteen-hour journey that cost me about four dollars and would have been four times that in first class.

At 11 A.M., with three short blasts on the horn, the old and rather untidy steamer pulled away from the dock leaving astern the tall offices of the shipping lines and the cupolas of the Church of Saint Spyridon. We passed timber yards, warehouses, and frigates of the Greek navy, and as we rounded the lighthouse on the end of the mole, music suddenly burst forth from a loudspeaker and a voice boomed *kalo taksithi* ("bon voyage"), to which the *Mioulis* replied with a short blast. Thus we headed out into the Aegean on one of those limpid blue days for which this sea is so famous, when Apollo himself seems to stride the skies. Behind us the town of Piraeus danced in the sun like washing on a line, until it dissolved into the misty brown hills of Attica.

There are approximately a thousand islands and islets in the Aegean (of which about one hundred are inhabited), so as you sail among them there are usually several in sight, looming out of the

◎◎ DEVIL'S ISLAND

blue, slipping past, and disappearing astern. They appear as low, misty, purple shapes on the horizon, but as you approach you can make out brown cliffs covered with green scrub and twisted trees. Small chapels are poised on isolated promontories, and white-walled villages sparkle in the distant hills like a sprinkling of snow. Each island has its own allure, and as you watch from the deck of the boat, it seems to return your gaze and beckon you to stay. For thousands of years boats have sailed the same waters, and millions of pairs of eyes have scanned the same jagged cliffs—yet a journey through the Aegean is one of personal discovery.

We put in briefly at the island of Melos, which I remember for its steep brown hills and the white-walled village perched on top. On most islands there are *choras* ("hill towns") similar to this; they were deliberately built in inaccessible positions as protection against the notorious Aegean pirates. Melos is best known for the Venus de Milo, which was found on the island in 1820.

It was night by the time we arrived at Ios, where the white buildings on the waterfront shone like moonstones. The tenders came out from the port, bringing with them a handful of new passengers and taking off an equal number of those disembarking. Crates and animals were unloaded into the tenders, and also two gleaming motorbikes that belonged to a couple of long-haired travelers from Los Angeles. I shall never forget those motorbikes. As they were being unloaded, the two youths were told that there are no motor vehicles or even roads on Ios.

Nobody can be prepared for arrival at Santorin. I had, of course, read about this "Entrance to Hades," so I was expecting the towering volcanic cliffs, the mule ride up the zigzagging path, and the smell of sulphur vapor. On a flat sea, in the dead of night, our

THE GREEK ISLANDS

boat sailed into the center of a huge volcanic crater, and we looked up at sheer rock cliffs nearly one thousand feet in height. On the topmost lip were the ghostly forms of houses and a scattering of lights—unfriendly lights, for in that strange place nothing could be familiar.

We were ferried ashore, and on landing we were set upon by surly muleteers, who grabbed for our luggage in an attempt to gain our business for the mule ride up to the top. I let myself be sold for thirty drachmas, which is just over a dollar, for though I could have walked up it in about half an hour, it would be ridiculous to come to Santorin and miss the famous mules. They are said to be possessed by the souls of the dead.

My anger at the rapacious behavior of the muleteers dissolved as we made the ascent. The moon threw a silver cast across the sea; the white houses above seemed to glow like luminous cardboard cutouts; and the sharp curses and whip snaps of the muleteers floated out onto the night. Santorin inspires both joy and hate.

A savage place! As holy and enchanted
As o'er beneath a waning moon was haunted.

The history of Santorin, as one would expect, is extraordinary. The island is the peak of a volcano, which over a period of thousands of years has erupted and changed its shape like a giant boil on the skin of the earth. Until about 1470 B.C. the island was circular and was called Stronghili ("Round"), but at that time a huge eruption spewed the insides out of the volcanic mountain and the sea poured in to fill the crater. Today the sickle-shaped island is one half of the volcanic peak, and the small island of Therasia to the west of Santorin is the other half.

◎◎ DEVIL'S ISLAND

In the center of the crater, where the sea is over one thousand feet deep, are three volcanic islets that are still changing shape, like living organisms. To visit the smallest of these islets, Nea Kaumene ("New Burnt Island"), as I did, is like arriving on the surface of the moon. There is no vegetation or habitation, and the surface is volcanic rock that varies in shape, color, and texture in different areas of the island. In places it is black and shiny and you feel that you are in a coal merchant's yard; elsewhere it is gray and more like a slag heap.

About twenty yards from where the boat landed there is a crater about fifty yards in diameter. Here the rocks are warm and coated with a yellow deposit like lichen, and sulphur vapor issues from deep cracks. Geologists say that there is no danger of another eruption on Santorin, but on Nea Kaumene one instinctively feels the reverse.

After the great eruption the history of Santorin follows a pattern that is similar to that of most of the Aegean islands. It was occupied by the Dorians and ruled over by a king, and in the fourth and fifth centuries B.C. it joined the first and second Athenian Alliances. It was used as a naval base by the Ptolemies in the war against Macedonia during the Hellenistic period, and in the Middle Ages it was occupied by the Venetians. From the sixteenth century until Greek independence in 1821 it was occupied by the Turks. During the Second World War Santorin was again occupied, first by the Italians (1941) and then by the Germans (1943); it was liberated in 1944.

In 1956 a catastrophic earthquake, which lasted forty-five seconds, left forty-eight dead, two hundred injured and two thousand houses in ruin. The villages of Oia and Pyrgos were almost

THE GREEK ISLANDS 🌀🌀

totally destroyed, and the main town of Thira (the old name of the island) was also severely damaged. Ruined and abandoned houses are still to be seen all over the island, and the population is said to have fallen from sixteen thousand to eight thousand.

Thira itself, which has been largely rebuilt, is an attractive, sparkling white town. The main street is beautifully quiet and is closed to all traffic, including donkeys. During the summer it is invaded by tourists, because the island has become a popular port of call for cruise ships. Perhaps the population of Santorin will begin to grow again with the increasing number of tourists who are flocking to the Aegean.

Beyond its massive ridge of cliffs, Santorin's vineyards and olive orchards slope down to beaches of fine black pumice three miles away to the west. From the rich volcanic soil grow the grapes that become the dusky, bittersweet wine from which the island gains most of its income. Water, incidentally, is at a premium, as it is on so many islands. Since there are no springs, rainwater has to be collected in cisterns, and in times of scant rainfall it is imported.

To the southeast of Thira is Mount Prophet Elias, a peak of 1,856 feet, on which there is a monastary and a radar station. On the headland beyond the peak are the ruins of the ancient city of Thira, which was the capital of the Dorian settlement. The site was excavated by wealthy Germans at the turn of the century, and some of the fine Hellenistic and Roman sculpture that was found there can be seen at the museum in Thira. The ruins themselves are not particularly impressive, but the old guardian amuses visitors by pointing out an enormous phallus etched into a rock and inscribed in Latin: "To my friends." He will also show the Festival Grounds, where youths danced naked at the festival of Apollo, and the stones

DEVIL'S ISLAND

on which they inscribed love messages to one another. It is a marvelous site for a festival, with the black volcanic beaches of Santorin stretching out on both sides of the promontory nine hundred feet below.

At Akrotiri, in the southern part of the island, archeologists are excavating a Minoan settlement that was destroyed by the great eruption in the middle of the second millenium B.C. The excavation looks like an untidy building site, with its trenches, heaps of earth and tin-roofed shacks, but the work going on here is particularly important because of the probable connection between the explosion of Thira and the collapse of the Minoan power on Crete at about the same time. It is thought that the eruption caused a tidal wave, as in the case of Krakatoa, that destroyed the Minoan palaces on the north of Crete.

Another theory is that the legend of the lost Atlantis is connected with the explosion and subsequent sinking of the island. It is a theory that has excited considerable controversy, and has yet to be proved or disproved. Though Plato's state of Atlantis is placed "beyond the pillars of Hercules," which would indicate the Atlantic Ocean, and dates from thousands of years before the eruption of Thira, Professor Marinatos of the University of Athens maintains that dimensions of time and space become distorted in myth and that the germ of the Atlantian legend could have been the sinking of Thira. Perhaps one day archeologists will dig up the answer; after all, Troy was a myth before it was found.

The *meltemi*, the north wind that prevails in the Aegean during the summer months, was at gale force the day I left Santorin. Waves crashed across the bows of the tender as it took us out to the ship, which was four hours late, and drawing alongside was a

THE GREEK ISLANDS

perilous operation. It was evening, and red clouds were billowing over the volcanic cliffs, evoking an image of that colossal eruption three and one-half thousand years ago.

Island of the Knights

Beach parasols, multistory hotels, a bevy of cruise ships—this was my first sight of Greece's most popular tourist island from the deck of the M.S. *Philippos*. Then, rounding the point, we were looking out along a line of massive walls, without breach or break, much as they appeared to the Turks when they laid seige to and finally overthrew the city in 1522.

"Nothing in the world was ever so well lost as Rhodes," wrote Charles V of Spain when he heard of that great military epic in which the meager forces of the Knights of Saint John of Jerusalem held off an enormous Turkish army for over six months. During the struggle nearly three-quarters of the Knights and an estimated eighty thousand Turks were killed. The fortress, built by the Knights and occupied by them for two centuries, fell only after they were betrayed by one of their own men. When Sultan Suleiman the Magnificent finally broke through, he spared the lives of the Knights and allowed them to leave in peace. The last of the European Crusaders sailed for Crete and thence for Malta; the final battle in the long, costly, fruitless wars of the Crusades was over.

Yet, in a sense, the will of the Knights finally triumphed, for in spirit at least they have never left Rhodes. Their buildings and

THE GREEK ISLANDS

massive fortifications have been so well restored that the City of the Knights in the upper part of the town is very much like it was during the Middle Ages. Here can be seen the Streets of the Knights, bordered by the inns of the various nations that made up this international order of religious warriors, and the Palace of the Grand Master, which the Italians reconstructed inside with the intention of making it into a palace for Mussolini. The Italians also faithfully restored the Hospital of the Knights, where the sick were said to have received their food on silver platters; today it is a museum.

The Turks, on the other hand, left few traces after nearly three centuries of occupation. A few fountains and mosques, a cemetery, a small Turkish community, and a Turkish bazaar atmosphere in the narrow, lively streets of the old quarter of town are all that survive. Perhaps there is more, but the Greeks prefer to forget those bleak years.

During the Golden Age, Rhodes was for a time one of the most prosperous islands in the Mediterranean. It was a center of trade between Italy, Greece, Asia and Africa; its currency was widely accepted, its sailors known for their bravery, and its maritime law contributed much to the international law of today. A symbol of its power was the Colossus of Rhodes, a one hundred-foot bronze statue of the Sun God, Helios, one of the seven wonders of the ancient world. It was built in 280 B.C., but fell during an earthquake fifty-six years later and lay in ruins for eight hundred years, until it was taken away by the Saracens and melted down. Nine hundred camels were required to carry away the broken pieces.

One is reminded of classical Rhodes when one goes to Lindos, one of the three great ancient cities of the island. The pretty road

◉◉ ISLAND OF THE KNIGHTS

from Rhodes passes by orchards, meadows and rocky mountain ridges that bristle like hair on a dog's back. About thirty miles from Rhodes the road suddenly climbs; below is a shimmering peacock-blue sea studded with golden cliffs. Perched on top of a sheer pinnacle, like a crown, are the slender, honey-colored columns of the Temple of Athenia Lindos, one of the great classical monuments of Greece. Surrounding the temple are the crenelated walls of a Byzantine fortress, and below is the sparkling white village of Lindos.

Shortly after taking in this breathtaking view, I was sitting on the marble stones of the temple looking down a four-hundred-foot precipice into the depths and shadows of the sea. Helen of Troy visited this temple and left a cup in the shape of her breast as an offering—we come with our cameras and take what we can of the scene and leave nothing as a tribute to its beauty.

On the summit of the citadel of Lindos, thou art
O Athena the glory of this ancient city.

Rhodes, "beautiful as the sun itself," is the complete island. It has everything to attract tourists in thousands: fine beaches, sailing and skin-diving facilities, history and antiquities, a modern town with luxury hotels and nightclubs, and good shopping because it is a free port.

Rhodes is also five times larger than any other island of the Dodecanese, "Twelve Islands," though there are in fact about forty islands in the group. They were once known as the "Privileged Islands" because of certain favors they received from the sultan; eventually they were the least fortunate of the Greek islands, because Turkish rule lasted longer here than anywhere else—until

THE GREEK ISLANDS 〰️〰️

1912. Even then they did not become united with Greece, because they were seized by Italy in the Turkish-Italian War. The Italians controlled the islands through World War II, and they were finally reunited with Greece officially in 1947. Today most of the old people in the Dodecanese speak Italian.

Kalymnos is the fourth largest island of the group, and it is the very absence of antiquities and monuments that is the chief attraction of the island; because there is nothing much to see, very few tourists go there. Ovid describes Kalymnos as "shaded with woods and fruitful with honey." Today the woods are gone, as they are on most of the islands, leaving barren mountains and rich, fertile valleys full of vineyards, fig trees, and olive and orange groves.

The port and main town of the island, known both as Kalymnos and Pothia, is only a century old and therefore not particularly interesting from the architectural point of view; nevertheless its terraces of pastel-colored houses climbing steeply up the hill are most attractive. On some islands, Mykonos for instance, all the houses are painted white, but the Kalymnians are much less inhibited with their colors, painting walls, roofs, shutters, doorways and steps in all sorts of shades. There was a variation from this pattern during the Italian occupation—most of the houses were painted simply blue and white, the Greek national colors.

The island's chief source of income is sponge diving, for which it has been famous since classical times. The fleet puts out each year in the spring, usually just after Easter, and while I was on the island I saw the boats being painted and made ready for voyages of six months or more that would take them as far as the shores of North Africa.

In former times the diver's equipment consisted of a face mask

ISLAND OF THE KNIGHTS

and a trident, but today he uses a diving suit or aqualung. Accidents are said to have been alarmingly numerous in recent years, because the intrepid divers often ignore some of the basic rules of diving and stay below the surface far beyond the prescribed time and surface much too quickly. This is a result not only of ignorance but of pride: for the diver it becomes a point of honor how long he can stay down and how many sponges he can bring up.

One could easily spend a lifetime visiting the islands of the Aegean. I should have liked to visit more of the Dodecanese: the little island of Patmos, for instance, the exile home of Saint John the Divine, where he was inspired to write *Revelations*; Kos, the second largest island and the birthplace of Hippocrates, the first doctor. These islands will have to wait for a second trip. From Kalymnos I went south to Crete, where I had arranged to spend Easter, the festival of festivals in Greece.

The Great Island

Out in the dark blue sea there lies a land called Crete, a rich and lovely land, washed by the waves on every side, densely peopled and boasting ninety cities.

Thus Odysseus describes Crete in the *Odyssey* at a time when the island possessed colonies throughout the Aegean, and tributes were sent from Athens to the Minoan kings. Today, Crete is a poor, sparsely populated island, and its three largest towns, Iraklion, Rethymnon, and Khania, are ramshackle, dusty places with a combined population of a little over one hundred thousand. Yet Crete is an island of great beauty, with fertile valleys, snowcapped mountains and a people who are justly renowned for their hospitality, bravery, and fierce pride. It is not without reason that the Greeks still call Crete the Great Island.

I arrived in Iraklion on Good Friday, when the long drama of Easter was coming to a climax. In the Orthodox calendar, Easter, the most important event of the year, falls about a month after the Roman Catholic and Protestant Easter. It is not just a short religious holiday. On Ash Wednesday, the most devout Christians begin a strict fast during which meat, fish, eggs, cheese, and even

THE GREAT ISLAND

olive oil are prohibited. For others, fasting begins during Holy Week, when religious activities become increasingly intense: long services are held each night in churches throughout the country, and preparations are begun for the Easter feast that will mark the end of the fast at midnight on Holy Saturday.

In Kalymnos at the beginning of Holy Week there was no meat in shops or restaurants, and fatted lambs, their heads painted with red dye, were being sold in the marketplace ready for slaughter on Saturday. All the people I spoke to, young and old, men and women, were fasting to some extent.

Good Friday is a day for visiting the graves of relatives, a day of deep mourning. Flags were at half-mast in Iraklion, and offices were closed. I noticed effigies of Judas Iscariot swinging from the gables of some houses. The point of deepest grief came in the evening when a candle-lit procession paraded through the streets bearing the symbolic body of Christ.

I found this an impressive and spectacular sight. The sidewalks and the balconies of the houses along the route were crowded with people holding lighted brown candles, and in the distance was the sound of a brass band, which became louder as the cortege approached. At the head of the procession was a military band, and following were choirboys in flowing white robes, bearing church banners and flaming torches. Then came the long-bearded priests with their golden robes glittering in the flickering light. Following the priests was the *epitaphos*, a bier covered with a white embroidered cloth, symbolic of the body of Christ. This was carried on four strong shoulders, and behind it was the heavy cross of Christ followed by more choirboys carrying icons and treasures of the church. Last came throngs of people with lighted candles. Thus

THE GREEK ISLANDS 🌀🌀

was the body of Christ carried from Calvary to the sepulcher, through the streets of Iraklion and elsewhere in similar processions throughout Greece.

The next day the markets were pandemonium. Butchers were doing a roaring trade selling gory lamb carcasses with hideous, staring eyeballs, said to be the greatest delicacy of the animal. Long white candles decorated with ribbons were being sold hand over fist. The long ordeal of Easter would soon be over.

At 11 P.M. bells peeled throughout the town. For the second time in two nights the streets were filled with people clutching candles. But this time the candles were white and unlit, and the people were hurrying to the churches. As midnight approached, the square in front of Ayios Titos church was a sea of people. It was unbelievably quiet—as if everyone were holding his breath. The climax of days of fasting and preparation had come. A miracle was expected.

From inside the church came the sound of chanting, and then the small flickering light of candles outside the door. The lights multiplied as the flames were transferred from candle to candle back into the crowd. *"Christos anesti"* said a voice over a loudspeaker. The miracle for which the people waited and suffered had occurred. Christ had risen. A wave of relief swept the multitude as if it might, after all, have happened. The square had become a carpet of candlelight. "Christ has risen!" the people say. "Indeed he has!" is the reply.

Then, quite suddenly, the crowd dispersed. Everybody hurried home to the Easter feast, which would continue into the early morning. People climbing in and out of buses and cars with lighted candles sheltered the flames with their hands, because if a candle is brought back home without going out it will bring good luck.

◎◎ THE GREAT ISLAND

I went to a restaurant with some friends where we ate *mayiritsa*, Easter soup consisting of the chopped heart, liver, and intestine of lamb. Rather to my surprise I found it delicious, as were the *kokorets*, (Easter buns). We drank beer and cracked red Easter eggs. When I returned to my hotel in the early hours of the morning, the acrid smell of incense and burning candles seemed to be lingering still in the night air.

Easter Sunday is the most festive day of the year in Greece. After the long fast the balance is restored in an orgy of eating and drinking. The celebrations are said to be most lively in the mountain villages of the mainland, where lambs are roasted on spits in the village square and everybody helps himself freely from giant barrels of wine.

I decided to go out into the country and, more by chance than intention, found myself in the village of Kamares in the foothills of Mount Ida. As ill luck would have it, a busload of tourists from Iraklion had also chosen the same village in which to spend their Easter Sunday, so we feasted together outside the local *taverna*, eating chunks of lamb with our fingers and drinking rough red wine. Some of the villagers danced in the main square for the benefit of the tourists, but without a great deal of enthusiasm, it seemed. I was happy when the tourist bus headed back along the bumpy road to Iraklion in the early afternoon.

I certainly had a good ration of ceremony in my first few days on Crete, for, after the tourist bus had left, a wedding was to take place, and the village seemed to take on a new life. The event was heralded by two musicians—playing the *laute* and *lyra*, traditional Cretan musical instruments—who headed a procession of guests as they passed through the village to the bride's house. Shortly thereafter,

THE GREEK ISLANDS

they returned to the church accompanying the bride, who was dressed in white and wearing lipstick—a rare thing to see on Greek girls.

If the traditional wedding procedure had been followed, the bride's dowry would have been carried on mule back from her house to the house of the bridegroom early that morning, and there would have been a party at the bridegroom's house the previous evening. But Easter had interrupted the usual pattern, and, unfortunately, my Greek was not good enough to find out exactly what had already taken place.

The wedding ceremony itself was informal—much less solemn than an English wedding. Friends, relatives, and children clustered round the couple as the priest read the service from a large red book, against a background noise of whispering and shuffling children. At one point during the service the couple sipped a glass of red wine, and I was half expecting them to let it slip to the ground and break; that is said to be a sign of good luck. It is also said that when the priest says "and the woman should fear the man," the bride sometimes steps on her husband's toes indicating her disagreement. As far as I could see, the bride was happy to let it pass.

The couple's union as man and wife was symbolized when the white wedding wreaths, made of lemon blossoms, were exchanged three times over their heads. These wreaths are considered sacred, and after the wedding they are placed next to the family icons. Such is their importance that a married woman will say on occasions, "By my sacred wedding wreaths I swear that..."

After the short ceremony was over, the relatives and friends filed past to congratulate the bride and groom. They dropped gifts of money onto a tray, and in return each guest was given sugar-coated

THE GREAT ISLAND

almonds. There are superstitions associated with these too; it is said that if a girl sleeps with them under her head for three nights she will dream of the man she will eventually marry.

Outside the church there were trays of food and wine, and in the village square there was dancing, led by the bride and groom. To my ear the music sounded oriental, the tune continually weaving back on top of itself without beginning or end. It was a slow and elegant dance, and the bride was dazzling in her white wedding dress.

As afternoon turned to evening, young men danced in place of the wedding party, which had returned to the bridegroom's house for more celebrations. The music became faster and the dancing swift and sharp. The dancers were shepherds, sailors, workers from Athens—some lived in the village and some had come back for the Easter celebrations. They jumped in the air and slapped the soles of their shoes; they pranced like animals and danced so that the veins stood out on their glistening foreheads. It was as if the musicians had been playing in their sleep earlier in the afternoon; now they were awake, their eyes sparkled and their instruments jumped with life on their knees. They played the *pendazolis*, the Cretan warriors' dance, and the lead dancer leaped up to the height of his own shoulder. The music seemed to rise up out of the ground and echo into the mountains, where in the fading light I could just see the snow on the slopes of Mount Ida. In those brief moments of dusk I felt that I had glimpsed the soul of Crete.

There are no trains on Crete, but there are many buses, which wind their way perilously round the sinuous roads, laden with peasants and vegetables, priests and schoolchildren in blue uniforms. There are bluff-bowed fishing boats that connect the isolated villages on the rugged, sparsely inhabited southern coast. And there is a large population of donkeys and mules, which have a habit of stopping dead in their tracks and bellowing with such force that their bodies seem to be about to explode, and one sees why they have a reputation for being possessed by the spirit of the devil. In Crete you hiss to make a donkey move and vibrate your lips to make it stop, but the animals are no less obstinate than they are elsewhere in the world.

The most pleasant way of traveling, if you have the time, is on foot, and spring is the best time of year, for then the words of the Cretan song come true:

> *Crete, my beautiful isle, a flower-strewn garden,*
> *There's no other place like you in the world.*

There are said to be over fifteen hundred different plants and herbs on Crete, of which over a hundred are peculiar to the island. These include the famous dittany, which ancient writers mention as an effective pain-killer and which the wild Cretan goat is said to eat when hurt.

As you pass through country villages, the men sitting at tables outside the cafes will hail you: "*Hellas. Kathiste.*" ("Come. Sit down.") They will ask you who you are and where you have been and where you are going. And they will offer you *tsikouthia*, a strong Cretan spirit similar to schnapps, or mountain tea that is made from a variety of wild herbs. You will be served *mezethes*, consisting perhaps of raw artichoke or snails.

Invariably there will be somebody who has lived in America. Their stories tend to sound the same. "Lived for twenty years in the States, fella," said one old man I met in a mountain village.

◉◉ THE GREAT ISLAND

"Had my own restaurant in Cleveland. Anybody says anything against the States I tell 'em it's the best country in the world. You can make money over there. Had my own car, television and house. All the young men leave this place. They go to Athens, Germany, States, Australia. What can you expect?" I looked out over the valley where the evening sun shed gold on the barley fields and women on donkeys were bringing the goats into the village. It is easy to be romantic. "Poverty," the old man said. "That's all we've got here. Poverty."

Another favorite topic of conversation among the Cretans is the war, which they remember as if it happened only yesterday. Many books have been written about the resistance and the Melame landing when Cretan men, women and children fought the German paratroopers with primitive firearms, stones, and farm implements. Now, for the first time in centuries, the Cretans have no enemy, though it is sometimes said that if there is another revolution in Greece it could well start here.

In the countryside you see few isolated houses, the farmers preferring to live in the villages and go out to the fields each day to work. But there are small chapels scattered all about the country, especially on mountaintops. Frescoed chapels alone number about eight hundred, most of them dating from the fourteenth or fifteenth century. It is pleasant to step inside the tiny barrel-roofed buildings, if only for some cool air. Icons, often very old, are painted on the wooden screen in front of the sanctuary and oil lamps hanging from the ceiling can be refilled from bottles of oil on the windowsill. There are many monasteries too, and here the traveler can usually find a bed for the night.

In Greek the word for stranger, *xenos*, is the same as that for

THE GREEK ISLANDS

guest, which partly explains why the Greeks are so hospitable. Nowhere is this hospitality more evident than in the remote areas of Crete. In fact, the traveler never needs to worry about finding somewhere to stay for the night. One afternoon, while walking in the hills near Limenes in southern Crete, I came upon a group of shepherds and their families shearing sheep in a cave. To them I was a total stranger, but they treated me like an honored guest, plying me with thick red wine and lumps of greasy lamb, which they had just roasted on a spit.

That evening I met one of the shepherds in the village *taverna*, and we drank *tsikouthia* together. His name was Manoles, and though our conversation had to be simple because of language difficulties, we established a friendship. Since I had nowhere to sleep he invited me to spend the night in the cave with the other shepherds—and the sheep. Wrapped in Manoles' thick woolen cape, I spent a comfortable night on a bed of sprigs and was awakened at five the next morning as the shepherds began milking the sheep. For breakfast I drank the sweet milk, as warm as blood.

It is thought that the first settlers on Crete dwelt in caves, of which there are a great number on the island. In the large ones, there are many branches, giant stalactites and stalagmites, and underground streams and rivers. Many have yet to be explored. The caves that were sacred and used as religious shrines are of great interest to archeologists. Zeus is said to have been born in a Cretan cave, though it is disputed whether his birthplace is the Dhiktaion Cave near Psykhro or the Cave of Idha. At Matala on the southern coast of the island the insides of caves have been carved into alcoves, fireplaces, and benches. They are thought to have been inhabited since very ancient times, and the Romans used them

THE GREAT ISLAND

as burial chambers. Recently they were repopulated by a group of hippies, but eventually the authorities evicted them on the grounds that the caves are important archeological properties.

"Probably the most spectacular adventure that Crete offers is a trip through the Gorge of Samaria. People who have made the excursion—and there have not been many apart from natives of the area—resort to all sorts of extravagances in their descriptions, and, even allowing for travelers' tales, it is a moving experience." This is how John Bowman's guidebook on Crete describes what is the longest, deepest, and narrowest gorge in Europe.

In fact, probably thousands of visitors to Crete have been down the gorge, though on the day I made the seven-mile walk I saw no other person. The only sounds I heard were the roar of the river, the echoing cries of birds high up on the rock face, and sudden rushes of wind. I started at midday, which is really too late, for it is best to have a whole day to walk down the gorge to the sea.

As I made the descent, it was tempting to stop every few minutes to gaze into the misty space between the mountains and listen to the muffled sound of the water below. At the bottom of the gorge—twenty-five hundred feet or two hour's walk from the top—there are trees, a river, lush green grass, and an enchanted stillness. There I swam in the crystal water and drank for the pleasure of the taste.

About two miles into the gorge is the deserted village of Samaria, now nothing more than a few stone houses in a state of ruin. Shortly beyond Samaria the river disappears underground, and one continues along the dry riverbed consisting of boulders that are smooth and white—and very tiring to the feet. I was fascinated by the continually changing surface of the cliffs: in some places they are faceted like crystal and elsewhere pitted like pumice; their colors

THE GREEK ISLANDS 🌀

are a collage of browns, reds, oranges, blacks, grays, and whites.

The gorge is the natural home of the Cretan wild goat, but they are seldom seen because they stay high up in the cliffs and are fearful of human beings. The gorge is also full of a great variety of shrubs, herbs, and flowers. I was fascinated by a strange purple lily that gave off an evil smell. Each time I passed one it seemed to be staring at me as if a human being were trapped inside. I wondered if this was the hyacinth that came into being when Hyacinthus was killed (accidentally) by Apollo, for this is also said to be large and purple. Out of curiosity I dissected one and found dead insects inside, which convinced me that it was an evil flower. I christened it the Flower of Medusa, and I cleaned my knife thoroughly, fearing it might have poison on it.

By about four o'clock a premature twilight had descended on the gorge, and the towering walls seemed to be inching closer together. I had been taking my time, stopping now and then for photographs, and I began to fear that I might not reach the mouth of the gorge by nightfall. In places the sheer cliffs hover a thousand feet overhead, and at one point they are only ten feet apart, so that looking upwards is like peering up a chimney. The river, which had emerged from its subterranean passage, had become icy, and in the narrow parts I had to wade through it up to my calves. The early darkness had created an unreal world, and I saw why writers have compared the journey down the gorge to a descent into Hades, and why the Cretans of this part of the island believe in vampires.

It was nearly night when oleander bushes indicated that the sea was near and I emerged from the strange underworld into the semi-deserted village of Ayious Roumeli. A bottle of *retsina* and a meal of eggs and potatoes, all that was available, were very welcome, and

🌀 THE GREAT ISLAND

I slept soundly on a temporary bed in the cafe among the bottles of liquor and an unlocked cash drawer. There are no roads, of course, to Ayious Roumeli, and unless one is prepared to walk back up the gorge or along the steep coastal cliffs, the only way out is by boat. I had to spend two nights in the *kapheneon*, on a steady diet of eggs, potatoes, and corned beef, until a small fishing boat took me around the coast to the neighboring village of Chora Sfakion, where I caught a bus back to Khania.

In such a short space it is impossible to do justice to an island as rich and varied as Crete, just as it is impossible to describe the various places and things of interest that I saw within the short time of three weeks. Among many memorable experiences were a visit to the grave of Nikos Kazantzakis in Iraklion; the descent into the Dhiktaion Cave; a night spent in a monastery in Acrotiri; a visit to a marvelous little museum in Khania, where I had the pleasure of actually wearing for a few seconds the spectacles that belonged to the great Cretan statesman Venizelos; and, of course, various evenings at *tavernas*.

The biggest omission is the famous Minoan sites of Knossos, Phaestos, Malia, and Ayious Triada, which I have left out not because I found them uninteresting—on the contrary, they are among the most worthwhile things to be seen on Crete—but because they have been dealt with at length in many other books. The layman can only marvel at the sophistication of the art and architecture of the "most modern of ancient civilizations," in Sir Arthur Evans's words. The Minoan ruins do not take one's breath away by their grandeur, as do those of Angkor Wat, or the Parthenon, or the pyramids of Egypt. Rather they are interesting for the curiosity that they excite, the puzzles that lie under each stone.

1. *Spring flowers* and olive trees on ▶ Corfu, the most beautiful and populous of the Ionian Islands off the west coast of Greece; there are about four million olive trees on Corfu, which is famous for its oil.

THE GREEK ISLANDS

The Minoan civilization touches little on Cretan life today other than by attracting tourists to the island. It is meaningless to relate present-day Cretans to the Minoans of four thousand years ago. And if one sees, as I did, a beautiful girl with almond-shaped eyes like those of Minoan ladies in the frescoes of Knossos, she probably has Turkish blood. For it is the Venetians and Turks, who occupied the island for a total of over six centuries, that have left their marks —marks that can be seen not only in the architecture and customs but also in the heroic spirit of resistance that the oppression engendered in the Cretans.

Crete has almost always lived in a climate of rebellion, and its history is full of heroes and abortive revolts. "Freedom or Death" was the cry during the bloody years of revolution against the Turks, and usually it was death. The story of the monks of the monastery of Arkedi, who blew themselves up, and the Turks with them, has become a legend, as has the bravery of the Cretan resistance during the last war. These are a demonstration of the Cretan heroic ideal of *levendia*, which is illustrated in two lines of a Cretan song.

> *Man's courage is the only true wealth;*
> *Eat, drink and enjoy this deceitful world.*

Here, perhaps, is a key to the Great Island.

2. *Donkeys* are the standard means of transport here in Corfu, as they are throughout Greece; they are usually ridden sidesaddle.

3–4. *Painted houses* in Sinarades, a village well known for its wine and olives; the rugs hanging from the windows are hand-woven.

◀ 5. *Tenement flats* in this Corfu town are reminiscent of the slums of Naples; the island was under Venetian control for over four centuries (1386–1797), and Italian, once the official language, is still widely understood.

6. *Cricket* is played in Corfu, a heritage from the British who ruled the island from 1815 to 1864.

◀ 7. *Tiled roofs* of the village of Lakones and the cliffs of Palaiokastritsa on the west coast of Corfu.

8–9. *The cliffs* of Santorin (*overleaf*), in places 1000 feet in height, are the lip of an extinct volcano. Above, sulphur-coated rocks on an uninhabited islet indicate volcanic activity in the past.

10. *The town* of Santorin, or Thira as it is officially called, has been restored after a severe earthquake in 1956; it has recently been suggested that Thira is the site of the legendary state of Atlantis.

11. *The mules* of Santorin are believed to be possessed by the souls of the dead. There are six hundred steps up this path to the clifftop.

12. *A view* of the east side of Santorin; the island is famous for its grapes and wine.

13–14. *The ruins* of ancient Thira, on the south coast of the island, overlook black pumice beaches (*opposite*); this was the ancient Dorian capital of the island and the site of festivals in honor of Apollo.

15–16. *The Lion of Venice* sits proudly in the courtyard of the Hospital of the Knights on Rhodes; the building is now used as a museum. The Venetians ruled most of the Aegean for about three centuries, though they held Rhodes only briefly. After the Venetians, Rhodes was taken over by the militant Knights of St. John of Jerusalem who remained for two centuries.

17–18. *The Street of the Knights* is bordered by the inns of the various nations from which men set out for the Crusades; the escutcheons of the knights are above the doorways where the sketchers are sitting.

19. *A Byzantine font* in the old city of Rhodes. ▶

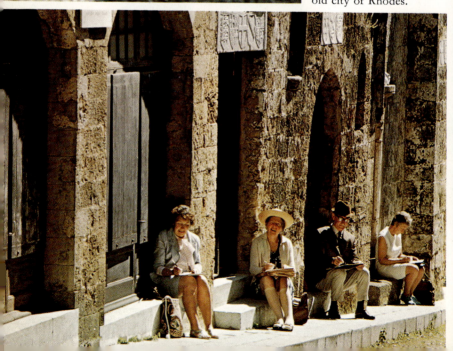

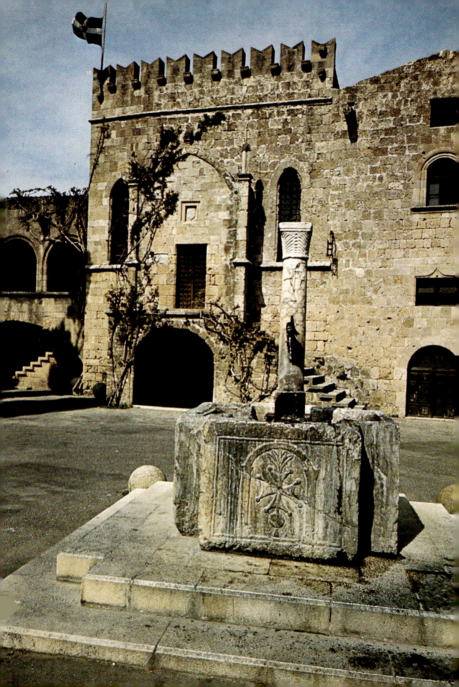

20–22. *The acropolis* of Lindos on Rhodes is one of the great classical monuments of Greece; once the most important city of the island, Lindos is now a village of about one thousand inhabitants, most of whom make their living from the tourist trade.

23–24. *Kalymnos,* the third largest of the Dodecanese islands, has been a sponge-fishing center since ancient times. Boats put out in early spring to seek sponges as far away as the North African coast, and they return in autumn. The demand for sponges has been hurt by the manufacture of synthetic substitutes.

25. *Children* of Kalymnos playing with lambs; behind is the port of the sponge-boat fleet.

26. *A letter* home is read by a friend. Many young men leave the islands to seek their fortunes overseas, and money sent home by them just offsets Greece's poor trade balance.

27. *An old man* in Kalymnos carries lilies for Easter decorations; many men on the island age prematurely because of the rigors of diving for sponges.

28–29. *Attractive children* are seen everywhere on the islands, and usually they are eager to have their photograph taken.

30. *These sheep* painted with dye in the marketplace at Kalymnos will shortly be killed for the Easter feast.

◀31. *Fishermen* in search of octopus use a glass-bottomed can to survey the seabed.

The Circle of Islands

From the summit of Mount Kynthos, the ruins of the ancient city were spread out below like the scattered fragments of Apollo's bones. It was early morning and the tiny island of Delos was deserted. The only sounds were those of the sea and the hollow ringing of sheep bells. In the distance the surrounding islands looked like sleeping dolphins, while Rhenea, which almost touches Delos, resembled a giant octopus stretched out on its belly on a sheet of shimmering blue steel.

Besides the ruins there is nothing on Delos except a small restaurant, a museum and a half-dozen cottages. Most visitors stay a few hours and return to the hotels, expensive restaurants, and night clubs of the neighboring island of Mykonos. But I wished to see Delos in the early morning, so I brought a sleeping bag with me and slept out in the open air. At dawn, after leaving my pack and bag at the restaurant, I made the short climb up what is grandiosely called "Mount" Kynthos. The view of the surrounding islands and the ruins is superb. One can see the Sacred Port, the Sacred Lake, and the marble lions that have stood guard over the city since ancient times. The rest is debris: snapped pillars, shattered colonnades, crumbling porticoes.

THE GREEK ISLANDS 🌀🌀

Delos is the birthplace of Apollo, God of Light, God of Music, God of Reason. According to the myth, it was on Delos that Leto, mistress of Zeus, found sanctuary. She was fleeing from the serpent sent by Zeus's jealous wife, Hera, and no island would receive her except Delos, which at that time was a free-floating rock. Characteristically, Zeus himself did not lend a hand, although he of course started the trouble. In due course Leto gave birth to twins, Apollo and Artemis, the virgin huntress. Delos's generosity was duly rewarded: four stout pillars grew up from under the sea and fixed the piece of rock to the seabed, thus establishing it as a proper island.

Delos became the sacred island, the greatest island in the Aegean. Pilgrims from all over the ancient world came to worship; they brought gifts of gold and silver, fine statuary and animals for sacrifice. Every four years there was a festival here, which is mentioned in the Homeric hymn to Delian Apollo: "Ionians in trailing robes are gathered together with their wives and children in thy streets; there they delight thee with boxing and dancing and song, making mention of thy name whenever they ordain contest." Until the end of the fourth century B.C. this was the greatest festival of Greece, and there were horse races, drama competitions, poetry contests dancing and feasting.

The rich built fine houses on Delos, and artists came to the island to make mosaics and sculpture. Under the Romans, Delos became a free port. It became rich, a trading center for grain and slaves. But the good fortune of the island did not last. In 88 B.C. Delos was invaded by Mithridatis of Asia, who destroyed the temples and fine buildings and slaughtered its twenty thousand citizens. Today only eight families live here; they guard the ruins and tend the sheep.

◎◎ THE CIRCLE OF ISLANDS

Delos is the center of the Aegean, or to be more precise, it is the center of the islands of the Cyclades, so-called because they form a kind of circle round the holy island.

To the north are the hazy blue bills and white sugar-cube houses of Tinos. The island has been called the Lourdes of Greece because of a miraculous icon that is said to have great healing power. Twice a year, in March and August, pilgrims and invalids flock to the island, and many are the stories of miraculous cures.

Separated from Tinos by a narrow strait is the large, mountainous island of Andros, which is fertile and wooded and resembles the mainland more than the other islands of the Cyclades. The island was once famous for its silk and for an annual bacchanalian festival, when the streams of the temple flowed with wine.

Almost equidistant from Andros and Kea is the barren islet of Giaros, formerly a refuge for pirates and bandits and today the site of a prison for political prisoners.

Kea is the northernmost of the western string of the Cyclades, poor, sparsely inhabited islands infrequently visited by tourists. In ancient times each had an importance and wealth far greater than it has today. Kea, which is rugged and mountainous, with a population of only seven thousand, boasted four cities. So great was the population on the island that there was a barbarous custom that people on reaching the age of sixty were expected to commit suicide. On the appointed day there would be a festival, and those who had reached the end of their life-span would be garlanded with flowers before they drank the deadly hemlock. There is also a story, quoted by Strabo, that once when Kea was beseiged by the Athenians, the islanders threatened to kill all their elder citizens. Faced with the prospect of such horror the Athenians retired.

THE GREEK ISLANDS 🌀🌀

Kythnos is another barren and mountainous island that has seen more glorious days. Its administrative laws were once famous throughout the Greek world and were expounded by Aristotle. The island is also known as Thermia because of the hot springs on the eastern coast.

The iron and copper mines of Serifos brought prosperity until the Middle Ages, and though there are still ironworks, the island is no longer rich. Few tourists come, though the sparkling white hill town is one of the loveliest in the Aegean.

One day I shall visit Siphnos, southeast of Serifos, whose gold and silver mines made it one of the richest places in the ancient Aegean world. It was also said to be an island of great beauty, "with meads enamelled with flowers and plains perpetually productive of fruit." Today the population is about two thousand.

Due west of Delos and clearly visible from Mount Kynthos is Syros, the capital of the Cyclades, whose port at Ermoupolis was the largest in Greece until the end of the last century. Today the port has a half-empty feeling, and the large, elegant houses and beautiful paved squares of the town speak of a vanished prosperity.

I have pleasant memories of a Sunday evening in Ermoupolis, when the main square was filled with Syriots taking their evening *volta* (promenade) and a military band played on the bandstand. There was an Edwardian elegance about the scene, the children in their Sunday best and groups of pretty girls stealing furtive glances at sailors in smart white uniforms.

To the southeast, just visible under a thin morning haze, are the twin peaks of Naxos and Paros. It was on Naxos, the largest island of the Cyclades, that Theseus left Ariadne on his return from Crete after slaying the Minotaur. The story is worth telling, perhaps,

THE CIRCLE OF ISLANDS

for it explains where the word Aegean comes from. The King of Athens, Theseus's father, had ordered that when his son's boat returned from Crete a white sail should be hoisted if he had been successful. But if he had failed, which would mean he had died, a dark sail should be left on the mast. In the excitement of the moment Theseus forgot the instructions, and when his father saw the dark sail, he threw himself into the sea from the top of the Acropolis. The King's name, Aegeus, became the name of the sea.

With a powerful telescope it might be possible to see the port of Naxia and to pick out the clean white lines of the gate of the Temple of Apollo, which stands on the edge of the sea overlooking the town. This marble gate, the well-known symbol of Naxos, is frequently depicted on the stage set for Richard Strauss's famous opera, *Ariadne auf Naxos,* and this may explain why a large proportion of the tourists who go to Naxos are German. It is appropriate that the gateway stands on top of the ruins of the temple of Dionysus, for it was Dionysus who found Ariadne shortly after Theseus had deserted her.

The Naxians believe that Dionysus was born on their island, which perhaps has something to do with the goodness of the wine and the excellence of the liqueur, Citron. According to one eloquent Naxian, "In Citron you hold within your mouth the quintessence of a lemon grove, the pale breasts of the fruit, the dark green of the leaves, and the perfume which rises from the bruised peel." Understandably the Naxians are enthusiastic worshipers of Dionysus.

Unlike the other islands of the Cyclades, Naxos is green and fertile, resembling somewhat the northern Sporades or even the Ionian Islands. Olives and grapes and other fruits and vegetables

THE GREEK ISLANDS 🌀🌀

grow abundantly, as do seed potatoes, which are sold to Ireland, of all places.

During my stay on the island I took a bus into the hills to the village of Apiranthos, a large white-walled village whose streets are paved with white marble. This is not as strange as it might sound, for Naxos once had many marble quarries.

I remember the village particularly for a small, dark and dusty museum where I saw Cycladic art for the first time. There was not much: flat stones etched with strange dots and spirals, like motifs in a drawing by Paul Klee; tiny marble female figurines in cubist style, looking as if they had been designed by Picasso; stylized heads also in a cubist style. These were made on Naxos about five thousand years ago, yet great artists of today are still striving for the same primitive perfection. Later I saw much more Cycladic art in the museum in Athens, but I was happy that my first contact with it came in a small village in the mountains of Naxos, one of the islands where it flourished.

I left Naxos as I left nearly all the Greek islands—wishing that I could have stayed longer. I should have liked to have seen the unfinished *kouros* of Apollo, and I should have liked to spend more time in Naxia itself. It is an attractive town, most of the houses being of the characteristic rounded Cycladic form, but there are also traces of the Venetians who occupied the island for three hundred years, leaving behind their coats of arms above some of the doorways, a small Roman Catholic community that still survives, and the Lion of St. Mark, now crumbling with age.

West of Naxos, across a narrow and often turbulent strait, is Paros, a pretty island about half the size of Naxos with a charming white town surrounded by green hills. Paros is a popular tourist

THE CIRCLE OF ISLANDS

island, though far less so than Mykonos or Rhodes. On a line from Delos passing between Paros and Naxos is the island of Ios, which, together with Melos, Folegandros, Sikinos and Amorgos, forms an arc of the less frequented islands; they are the outer circle of the Cyclades. Directly south of Ios, and well outside the Cycladic circle, is Santorin.

About five miles east of Delos is Mykonos, the "Capri of the Aegean." In spite of the masses of tourists who crowd the waterfront and beaches during the summer season—ranging from the rich and famous to long-haired wayfarers with rucksacks and guitars—the island is one of the most charming in the Cyclades.

As one approaches, it seems nothing more than a brown, barren rock speckled with whitewashed houses. Drawing nearer, one can see the red and blue cupolas of the churches, the gaily painted caïques and the famous round, thatched windmills. On the quay to meet the ferry are always a covey of middle-aged women looking for people to rent rooms to. "Room! Room!" they say, for it seems that this is the only English word that some of them know. Rooms in private houses in the islands are cheaper than hotels, and from my experience much more pleasant.

Walking through the narrow streets of Mykonos is like being in a snowstorm. Everything is painted in blinding white, even the cracks between the paving stones, and in the early morning the Mykonots can be seen outside their houses performing this ritual of purification. The streets of the town are so narrow and the maze of alleys so confusing that once you have found a room there is a danger of never being able to find it again; it is said the streets were made this way to confuse the pirates.

The architecture on Mykonos is delightful: domed churches and

32. *A goatherd* leads his goats across
the Omalos Plateau in southwestern
Crete. There are very few cows on the
island, but the many sheep and goats
provide meat, wool, milk, and cheese.

THE GREEK ISLANDS

squat, irregularly shaped houses that have wooden balconies and outside staircases. The island is said to have as many churches as there are days in the year, which works out roughly at one for every ten people. Many of them have been built by sailors to honor pledges made in storms. Some are no bigger than kennels, and one is so small that it is called the Church of Cat. The most famous, the Church of Paraportiani, inspired many of the designs by the architect Le Corbusier.

At one time Mykonos was considered an ill-favored place and the poverty of the islanders was proverbial. Ovid wrote of "humble Mykonos," and Strabo says that all Mykonots go bald at the age of twenty or twenty-five. The island was also well known for the passion with which the dead were mourned. At the end of the last century J. Bent wrote: "Everywhere in the Cyclades we were told that when we came to Mykonos we should hear the best lamentations over the dead that exist in Greece: that barren Mykonos had this one unenviable speciality; nowhere else could the wailing women sing over the dead with such stirring, heart-rending dirges as there. So we went to Mykonos with the firm determination of waiting until somebody died." He then goes on to describe the ecstasies of grief, the tearing of hair, and the beating of breasts. There are still professional mourners in Greece, though they are not as violently emotional as they were.

In contrast, Mykonos today is the gayest of all the islands, and there is an abundance of hotels, restaurants, boutiques, and nightclubs that brings prosperity to the islanders. The Mykonots seem to be on the whole happy and friendly, and the life of foreign residents there, as one American told me, tends to be an endless party. For myself, Mykonos is fine for a weekend—like champagne it

33. *The White Mountains* of Crete rise over 8000 feet. Two-thirds of the island is barren and mountainous.

34. *The village* of Kamares nestles in the foothills of Mount Ida.

35. *A wedding procession* in Kamares, preceded by two musicians, leads the bride from her house; the man in front plays the three-stringed *lyra*, an old Cretan instrument.

◀36. *Candles* are decorated with blue and white ribbons for Easter.

37. *An old woman* in Kamares.

38. *A holy book* held by the priest is kissed by a villager.

39. *Dancing* in the village square after the wedding.

◀40. *Venetian houses* overlook the deserted outer harbor of Khania, the capital of Crete; ships now dock at nearby Souda Bay.

41. *Derelict* windmills at Elounda in northeastern Crete; shards of pottery abound in these fields that were the site of a Minoan settlement.

42. *The Palace of Knossos* was excavated at the beginning of this century to reveal traces of the hitherto unknown Minoan civilization that flourished in the second and third millennia B.C. Because of its complexity, the palace itself might have been the labyrinth in which was kept the Minotaur that was eventually killed by Theseus.

43. *The Throne Room* at Knossos.

44. *Bull-leaping* depicted on a fresco at Knossos.

45. *The double-axe* symbol on this jar is a recurring and puzzling motif in Minoan art.

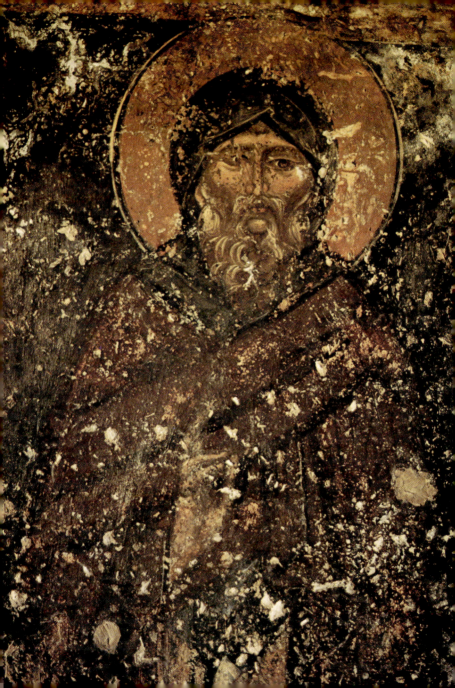

46–47. *Byzantine* frescos decorate some of Crete's many churches and chapels; left, a fourteenth-century fresco, a fine example of the Cretan school, painted on the wall of a small country chapel in Spilia, western Crete.

48. *Our Lady of St. Roumeli Church,* at the mouth of the gorge at Samaria, was built by the Venetians in the sixteenth century.

THE CIRCLE OF ISLANDS

bubbles and froths for a short time and then becomes flat.

The caïques that take the tourists to Delos come from Mykonos; how different they are from the fleets of *theories* that came to the festivals in ancient times. From Athens and from various islands in the Aegean, they brought choirs and dancers and athletes, poets and philosophers, animals for sacrifice and horses for racing, and sumptuous gifts for Apollo. Festival day must have been something like a huge regatta, a pageant of colored sails and long-hulled boats whose banks of oars cut like teeth into the wine-dark sea. What a splendid sight it would have been then looking down from Mount Kythnos.

The Far Island

What can a man know who lives in a room?
Some men live in the world.
Some men go in boats to Youra.
There, maybe they can feel the sea recede
at night, and know
I cannot know.

From "Youra" by Ronald Silliman

I was awakened by the sound of footsteps on the deck above me. Looking up through the hatchway, I saw Giorgios by the engine lighting a screw of newspaper that he poked into the head of the cylinder. He cranked the flywheel and the engine cracked to life like a machine gun. He jumped to the quay to release the bow, pulled up the four-pronged anchor, accelerated the engine, threw over the tiller—and we were heading out of the harbor.

It was 4:30 AM. The small harbor of Patitiri was asleep under a white mist, and we were making for a patch of orange in the eastern sky, the first glimmerings of dawn. Giorgios swung a bucket into the sea and sloshed the orange decks with seawater, leaving the tiller to look after itself. It would be about five hours to Youra.

THE FAR ISLAND

The previous evening Giorgios, Tassos, a builder, Tony, an English writer, and myself had been sitting in one of the cafes overlooking the harbor of Patitirion Allonnisos. During the course of the conversation I had said that I would like to visit Youra, the island of caves and wild goats. No sooner was it said than it was decided that Giorgios would take me there the next day. We would have to leave early, he said, so towards midnight we had walked along the quay to his boat, where I slept soundly in the forecastle hold, which is normally used for storing fish.

Thus I found myself sitting on the deck of Giorgios's boat with the air blowing through my hair as we chugged up the rocky eastern coast of Allonnisos. Here green fir trees grow among the red rock almost down to the water's edge, and for most of the way there were no signs of human life. After about half an hour we passed a settlement of about eight houses that, said Georgios, is called Stenivali.

Suddenly the sun rose above the gray lip of a distant island. The air was so clear that I could see it from the moment it rose above the horizon and I would be able to see it throughout the day until it fell below the horizon again.

There are many uninhabited islands in this forgotten corner of the sea to the east of the northern Sporades, and some of them are quite large. In medieval times these waters were on an important shipping route to Byzantium, and Allonnisos was a prosperous island. The island was also a powerful pirate stronghold to which Barbarossa himself was said to have come to recruit men. Descendants of the pirate families still live on Allonnisos, though most of the island men are now fishermen or shepherds, and the population is only two thousand.

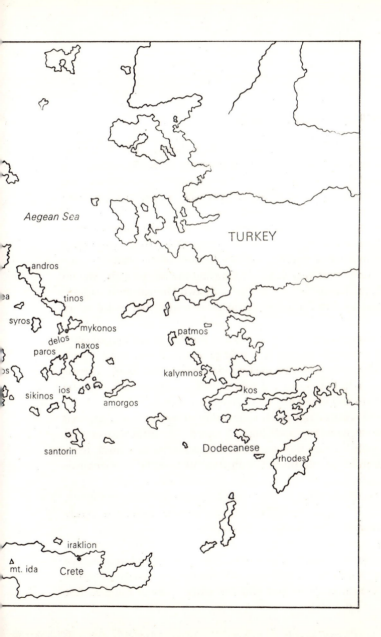

THE GREEK ISLANDS 🌀🌀

We passed the deserted island of Kiya Panaya. It is thought to have been inhabited at one time since various ruins, not yet properly excavated, have been found. Now there is just one monastery on the island, where an eccentric monk lives who is said to speak many languages. What a fate for a polyglot!

The fishermen say that there is a city under the water south of Kiya Panaya and also many sunken ships. One would expect there to be a number of wrecks, not only because of the pirates but because storms start very suddenly here and the jagged cliffs offer no protection. Tassos told me that recently two German treasure hunters came to dive for amphorae in these waters, but ended up in jail.

To voyage among these islands and stare up at the rugged cliffs, lacking any signs of life, is a strange and beautiful experience—very different from playing the Cyclades on crowded ferries. There is nothing here but occasional fishing boats, rugged cliffs, and the clearest sea and bluest sky that I have ever seen.

In fine weather not much seamanship or navigation is required in these empty waters, and Giorgios leaned against the small engine house with his bare foot on the tiller behind. He is a small, foxy-faced man in his mid-thirties, with thin fair hair and a broken pair of sunglasses that are held flat against his eyes with a piece of elastic; from one side it looks as if he is wearing a black patch like a pirate. Now he is singing Greek songs, just audible above the steady *tockatockatocka* of the one-cylinder engine.

The sun was already high by the time we got to Youra. It is nothing more than a steep crag of orange rock, dry and treeless. The cliffs drop into the limpid water like knives and descend fathoms below the surface. Giorgios said the water is about hundred feet

◎◎ THE FAR ISLAND

deep there. We tied up to a rock and ate bread, olives and large tomatoes before climbing up the steep path to the top of the cliff.

Three people live on Youra: Athanasias Kiriasis, the official keeper of the wild goats, his wife, and daughter. They have lived there for seven years. Their only contact with the outside world is through the occasional boat such as ours, that calls in from Allonnisos.

They greeted us warmly—Giorgios as an old friend—and we were invited into their clean, rather bare cottage, which reminded me of a crofter's cottage in the Scottish highlands. It is the only building on the barren island.

Athanasios, a lean dark man in his early forties, produced a ledger full of the names of the people who had visited the island during the past twelve years, and I estimated that there were several hundred, most of them Greek. I appeared to be the first Englishman in about five years.

After we had drunk *ouzo*, the five of us left the house to visit one of the large caves on the island. It is said to be the cave of the Cyclops where Odysseus and his men were held captive; they escaped by stabbing the giant's terrible eye with a stake and then hiding themselves under the bellies of sheep as they left the cave. The entrance is a narrow, horizontal slit in the gray rock, hardly big enough for giants to come in and out of, I thought. Inside it was dark and smelled strongly of goat. We lit candles and penetrated further. The cave is a forest of stalagmites and stalactites, as if it were formed by the dripping of giant candles over a period of centuries. Athanasios led us through a labyrinth of tunnels. He told us that the cave goes very deep and has never been fully explored. As we emerged I noticed big white rocks on the ground—the Cyclops's

THE GREEK ISLANDS

ammunition, perhaps, for driving off ships that ventured too near.

Although I did a lot of chasing over jagged rocks, I never got near enough to the wild goats to photograph them properly. Like the Cretan goats they are as nervous as deer and must be stalked accordingly. Athanasios said that the best time would have been early morning or late evening. I did, however, get a good view of one, a magnificent animal with horns the length of a man's arm and sticking out at right angles to its head.

Back at the cottage the two women prepared some beans, soft goats' cheese and wine. It was a simple and companionable meal. Later the three of them accompanied us to the top of the cliff. They waited as we climbed down the path to the water's edge. As we headed back towards Allonnisos I could still see them, standing like three statues on the clifftop.

49. *Caïque,* under construction in Spetsai; the island was one of the three most important naval ports during the Greek War of Independence and was the first to rebel against the Turks in 1821.

50. *Hydra,* like Spetsai, was a leading naval base during the War of Independence; in the eighteenth century it had the largest trading fleet in the Aegean. Today Hydra is a favorite haunt of writers and artists.

◀51. *Chris Louis* comes from Athens, but her family has a second home on Spetsai; the islands are being repopulated by wealthy Greeks and foreigners whose way of life is very different from that of the islanders.

52. *Skopelos* is a green and wooded island, rich in figs, plums, grapes, olives, almonds, and pears.

◄ 53. *This marble gateway* is all that is left of the temple of Apollo on Naxos; Theseus left Ariadne on this island, the largest in the Cyclades.

54–56. *The traditional costume* worn by islanders on Naxos; worry-beads are owned by most Greek men.

58–59. *Cycladic art* was being produced well before the Greek peninsula became important; made about five thousand years ago, their primitive shapes and figurations have been an inspiration to artists of today.

60. *Kouroi*, ceremonial statues of naked youths, were brought to Delos as gifts to Apollo. Some of them are among the finest examples of Greek art.

◀57. *In ancient times* fine temples and houses stood on the sacred island of Delos, the birthplace of Apollo, and there was a population of many thousands; today the buildings are in ruin and the island is inhabited by only a few families.

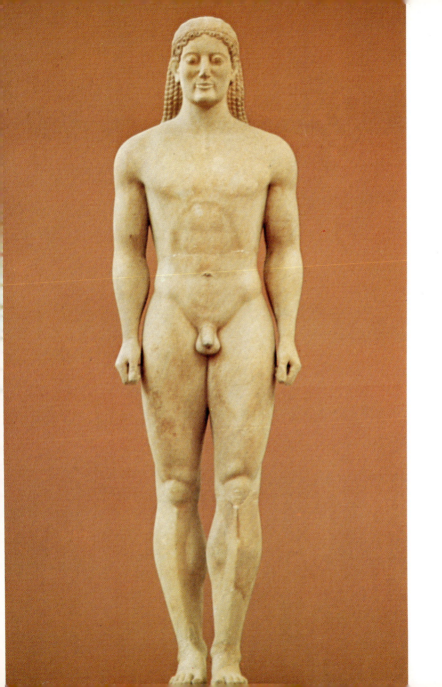

61. *Koukounaries* beach on Skiathos is reputed to be the finest in Greece; the green and fertile island is famous for its sandy beaches.

63-64. *Mykonos,* the most popular tourist island of the Cyclades, is said to have 360 churches, about one for every ten inhabitants; the streets were designed to confuse pirates.

◀62. *The cycladic* form of the Church of Paraportiani on Mykonos is said to have influenced the designs of Le Courbusier.

65–66. *Spotless whitewash* is the pride of Mykonos; even the streets are painted.

67. *Weavers* of Mykonos prosper through tourism; the island was once one of the poorest in the Aegean.

68. *Many private homes* offer accommodations to visitors at reasonable prices.

69. *Windmills* are the symbol of Mykonos.

70–71. *Athanasios Kiriasis,* his wife, and his daughter are the only inhabitants of the rugged island of Youra; he is the official guardian of a rare species of wild goat.

72. *A fishing boat* returns to port at sunset.

THIS BEAUTIFUL WORLD

- The Himalayas
- Palaces of Kyoto
- Peking
- Gods of Kumano
- Moscow
- Michelangelo
- Afghanistan
- Hawaii
- Seoul
- Goya
- The Alps
- The Acropolis
- Vienna
- African Animals
- Thailand
- Yosemite
- San Francisco
- Bali
- Spain
- Mexico
- Imperial Villas of Kyoto
- Journey through Africa
- The Grand Canyon
- California
- Mongolia
- Lapland
- The Greek Islands
- Hong Kong
- Angkor Wat
- Istanbul
- The Road to Holy Mecca
- Burma
- The Andes
- New Guinea
- Marketplaces of the World
- Traditional Tokyo
- Ireland
- Australia
- India
- Cherry Blossoms
- Okinawa
- New York
- London
- Sri Lanka
- Iran
- Yugoslavia
- Washington
- Rome
- Brazil
- Alaska
- Delhi and Agra
- Boston
- Malaysia
- El Salvador
- Venice
- St. Louis
- Philippines
- Cairo
- Florida
- Kashmir
- Kathmandu Valley
- Switzerland
- Touring Tokyo
- Singapore

In preparation
- Greater Los Angeles